The Fire Within

Transform Your Life

The Fire Within

Transform Your Life

Charles L Ellis

Printed in the United States of America
First Printing, 2018
ISBN-13: 978-1985024700
ISBN-10: 1985024705
TFW Publishing
San Diego, CA. 92154

"We lift ourselves by our thought. We climb upon our vision of ourselves. If you want to enlarge your life, you must first enlarge your thought of it and of yourself. Hold the ideal of yourself as you long to be, always everywhere."

Orison Swett Marden - 1850-1924, Inspirational Writer

"Charles Ellis is a caring and wonderful individual. I had the privilege of working with him a few years ago and his work ethic speaks volumes about his character. One topic-other than his wife's cooking-that always came up in conversation was his love for young people and his desire to help them rise to new heights and achieve their goals in life. He's the kind of guy you want to lend your ear to."

Wanda Anderson
MDiv, Author of End of the Robe

"Charles is kind, incredibly smart, very well read, and wise. His desire, passion, and determination in helping others and making this world better is refreshing. In The Fire Within, Transform your life, Charles endeavors to reach and help even more people change their lives."

-Susan Davis
Film Director, Business Owner

"I got to know Lamont about five years ago…We were talking about people who had made a difference in his life and he kept bringing up Charles Ellis, whom he called "Mr. Big Book". I said, "Lamont, what is so special about this Mr. Big Book"? He told me that Charles Ellis really cared about his (Lamont's) life, that he had never met anyone who stuck with him and was determined to be there for him no matter what. Just as we were talking, Lamont's cell rang. It was Mr. Big Book himself calling to check in with Lamont, something he did pretty much every day. I spoke briefly with Mr. Ellis who said it was just the way he did things. He never gave up on people and supported them for as long as they needed and wanted him in their lives. This is too rare a quality in these times. And it made all the difference in Lamont's life. Mr. Ellis was like the father Lamont never had. Loyalty, perseverance, trust, love. Nothing beats those qualities. Lamont's life was saved by Mr. Big Book staying there through thick and thin."

-Sue Hammond
Retired educator and counselor

Dedication

This book is dedicated to my wonderful wife Shawna.
She continues to support me, push me, believe in me,
while continuing to share this life of gratitude with me.

Contents

Acknowledgements

I write this book in hope that my passion for service in this world will be of benefit to and for my Children. So, thanks LaTasha, Crystal, Josephine, Tyquawn, and Shyla for being in this world. Each of you has an extraordinary capacity to impact the world and make it a better place. May the things I do become a blessing in your lives.

I also want to thank my friend and co-worker Michael who always puts the things I say to the test, gives me input, and engages in countless opportunities to question and discuss changing realities and transformation with me. I thank you to Gary Graham for always wanting to know more about The Fire Within and giving me the opportunity to explain it and also having the dedication and heart that's needed when it comes to helping the youth and young adults at work.

This book is also dedicated to the many individuals and supporting staff who work at The San Diego Job Corps, hoping to and making a difference in the lives of so many youth and young adults, and who make San Diego Job

Corps one of the top in the nation. Each of you has something to contribute to the success and future of this wonderful opportunity for our young people, who are ready to make this world a better place. Gratitude!

And a very large thank you to everyone I've met on this path and mysterious journey of changing paradigms. We are all teachers and students.

The stage is set and the actors in place. Go forth and enjoy this wonderful journey!

Foreword

Community, commitment, and service are needed to build relationships and help move our world forward into the future. Working toward these goals is the responsibility that we each need to share. At a time when more positive visions and ideas are needed, both for the individual and humanity as a whole, whenever something or someone carries the seed of enlightenment, then attention should be given.

Charles Ellis, contributes his passion for helping others to realize their dreams and understands that living a life of gratitude and service is possible as he uses his passion to help others by mentoring, coaching, writing, and just plain old listening. His approach motivates his clients and students to be productive while reaching for their ideal lives.

In The Fire Within: Transform Your Life, Charles has endeavored to help anyone who feels stuck in their old paradigms and negative cycles, understand that it is possible to live the life they envision and to find their yes. His idea is that each individual has a fire, which burns inside, waiting to express itself and give that special gift to the world. It encourages the reader to find their yes, believe in him/herself, reach for and obtain their goals while going through personal transformation.

It has been great to watch Charles go through the stages of instructional, motivational, inspirational, and finally transformational growth. I've enjoyed our meetings, exchanging of ideas, accomplishments, stories, and visions for the future. His dedication to inspiring the youth in our community and helping anyone hoping to create a better life is to be commended.

- Scott H Silverman- CEO/Owner of Confidential Recovery Author, Speaker, Coach, Mentor, CNN Hero Award Recipient

Introduction

This book is a continuation of my first book, The Fire Within: Right Here Right Now. Actually, that is not entirely correct. The Fire Within: Right Here Right Now was taken from this book's journey to completion. There is a fire within each of us which you may or may not be aware of. The ability to use this power is within each of us. The object of this book is to help anyone who is so inclined, to figure out and create their ideal life. Also, this is not just a positive thinking book. Yes, positive thinking has its place, which I will explain later, but this is about seeing what you want and thus creating what you want. This is a meditation process, and I couldn't imagine a day without meditation. There is just so much going on in our minds. For many people their thoughts are garbled and jumbled. More about thoughts later on.

This book is written in hope that you will begin to realize the power of belief and begin applying techniques which will help you on the road to your idea of success. I hope to give you something practical and understandable. As I wrote in my first book 'The Fire Within: Right Here Right Now', I believe that we are all capable of living our ideal lives. Not just a select few. The ideas and techniques in this book are not new, and in fact have attributed to more success and finances than you can probably imagine. It is my sincere desire that this book will help you understand, use, and thrive with the power of belief. I want you to reach your goals. This all starts with changing your thoughts or more so changing your belief system. Hopefully after reading this book you will understand or begin to understand your belief system and how it works. I'm writing this book with the desire that it will guide you to creating your ideal life or start you on that fabulous and mysterious journey. I've been paying a lot of careful attention to how extraordinary people make extraordinary things happen, and I am humbled just in the writing of this book, let alone that anyone will find it worthy of reading. This book was written in hope that it will help you unlock your full potential. I remember reading somewhere that "If you can think impossible thoughts, then you can do impossible things. How would you feel if you could be anything, have your heart's desires, and accomplish the things you want accomplished. Keep reading because you just may have taken the first step towards those goals.

It is my wish that you will have a profound shift in how you view reality or at least a little taste of what is possible should you examine the words I've written. It is my humble hope that you will begin to believe that anything is possible if you will but believe and change from that old paradigm that has maybe kept you in a rut, dead end job, unhealthy relationship, or perhaps low self-esteem which keeps you from making advances when you know in your heart that you should be growing and prospering. We all have an inborn purpose for being here, a dream to manifest, a story to tell, and a contribution to make. When I give a motivational or keynote speech, there is almost nothing more thrilling than to watch the eyes of someone glow when they GET IT, when the motivation begins to turn to inspiration. So, if you're ready to go forth and prosper, go forth and create, let's get started.

Chapter 1
The Fire Within

"At times our own light goes out and is rekindled by a spark from another person. Each of us has cause to think with deep gratitude of those who have lighted the flame within us."

Albert Schweitzer

In life there is so much conditioning from the world that a person doesn't usually know what to believe, what's real, or even how to go about being their true and authentic self. We may not even know that there is an authentic self, believing our thoughts, the labels given to us, our careers, our social status, or even what others tell us to be, as being who we really are. Nothing could be further from the truth. Even though society has conditioned us since birth, we still have that deep stirring within, telling us that there is so much more and that we should be doing so much more. As I wrote in my book The Fire Within: Right Here Right Now, the key to overcoming this dilemma is allowing this fire within to express itself and allowing this heightened state of emotion, expression, and authenticity to take the lead.

I believe one of the most important things we could ever do is to discover and unveil our authentic selves. It is not through money, success, and prestige that it is revealed, however, once we discover this fire within it could very well lead to those things. Uncovering who our authentic selves are is a wonderful process which leads to magnificent miracles in life. I believe that to be true alchemy. Ordinary everyday people become extraordinary and do extraordinary things. Actually, we are all magnificent and extraordinary, but most of us just don't know it. Getting to know yourself as extraordinary not only transforms you but the world around you. It begins with a willingness to acknowledge that there is something more, and the need to do something different than what you've been doing for most of your life. This becomes the beginning of living your life as the person you are meant to be. But fair warning, once you start on this path there is no turning back. You will be on your way to tapping into your True Self, your true power, and the YOU that is unique, individually special, and with qualities that make life a masterpiece. The fire within you can transform your passions into the dream, vision, job, career, and relationship that you desire. Are you ready to believe?

Chapter 2
The Fire Within: Belief

"If thou canst believe,
all things are possible to him that believeth"

Mark 9:23

So, let us get on with the process of believing. We each have a unique approach and perspective to the world. This is because of our beliefs. Belief is a built in system. This was developed as we were conditioned since birth. Through our experiences, events, places we've lived, etc. we've each developed a belief system. You have experiences and then your Belief System fills in the gaps, interprets it, tries to make sense of it, and ultimately influences your behavior. Actually, the reason that you believe what you believe is because you've practiced certain thoughts, over and over again. Again, beliefs are thoughts that you keep practicing. Whatever your dominant thoughts are will continue to attract like thoughts. The more you think those thoughts the more life will deliver more of them to you again and again and again. Actually, beliefs are one of the most powerful tools we have to shape our reality. In fact our whole life is built around our beliefs. Your self-limiting beliefs are the one thing that may be keeping you from living the life you dream of. Hopefully, by the time you finish reading this book, you will have a clear idea of exactly what you need to do to increase your potential for success in whatever you do. You will know how to trust and believe in yourself. You will also need to have a commitment to the process presented in this book. If you do this you will encounter a dramatic shift in how you see the world and how you live your life. My desire is that you will gain the tools along with the insight to completely transform your life. First, just know that you already have everything you will ever need. You just don't know it. You just haven't come to believe it. Without this understanding you will not be able to rise to your full potential. What most people don't realize is that there is infinite abundance. When you are lacking (or believe that you lack anything) it is because of your belief system. Your belief system is the cause of lack and shortages. Actually, there is more than enough for you, me, and everyone on this planet.

We each have core beliefs that are continuously running in our subconscious and contribute to how we live our lives every day. This unseen belief system determines how we see ourselves as well as the world we live in. Over and over again we affirm our thoughts, thinking them to be the truth of who we are and how things are. Most people never question their belief system. They just continue trying to justify their beliefs. They hold their beliefs up as if their identity is tethered to them. Changing your belief system gets you from where you are to where you want to go. Of course, any change requires persistence and repetition. Still, it is absolutely possible. Most of you may believe that you have to really work hard, or know someone, or be in the right place at the right time, and yet there is something else that is known to get you to where you want to be and that is your belief that you can and will. So I will suggest that seeing is not believing, but that believing is seeing. You attract to yourself health and success by how and what you believe. Most people may believe that the mind is powerful but usually have no idea just how mighty and powerful. That is why it has been said that if you can conceive it and believe it, you can achieve it. But no one can believe for you. That part is up to you. The great motivator and philosopher Jim Rohn put it like this, "You can't hire someone else to do your push-ups for you." They will be the only one getting the benefit. You will still be weak. Most of us know the quote by Henry Ford, "Whether you think you can, or you think you can't—you're right". Many sabotage their careers and their lives because they don't believe that they're deserving or some such self-defeating idea. They believe that they can't achieve their dreams or create their ideal lives. Most of us have our own self-limiting beliefs. We've been conditioned to blame other people, circumstances, the media, you name it, anything other than ourselves for whatever we don't like about our life. We put the blame everywhere except where the real problem lies which is within ourselves, within our very own paradigms. That's where the problem originates when it comes to manifesting the life you desire, and that's where we need to examine before we move forward. By the time you finish reading this book you may realize and uncover many negative self-beliefs and fears which you probably had no idea about. Once you change your belief system you change your reality and you change your thinking and behavior. You will still need to cultivate your belief system. Once you begin to train your mind to believe, your focus increases and you begin to understand that you create your own reality and that you have the ability to create your ideal life. We all have this great gift of being able to believe. It can lead to profound changes and shift your consciousness. Your beliefs are the blueprint for how you see the world and how you lead your life. We are always creating beliefs or finding ways to validate our beliefs. I wrote in my last book that paradigms do not like to change and when you attempt to change them, then you're in for a battle. It can be slow and difficult, yet it can and will get easier if you stick with it. Within our minds we have the astounding ability to create the reality that we want. And we are always creating, whether consciously or unconsciously. It's just that some people are more aware of this than others. My hope is that after reading this book you will have learned or on the way to learning how to deal with whatever challenge may present itself in your life. For too long most of us have been blind to the knowledge that we are responsible for what is happening in your life. Mahatma Gandhi has been noted as saying the following:

"Your beliefs become your thoughts.

Your thoughts become your words.

Your words become your actions.

Your actions become your habits.

Your habits become your values.

Your values become your destiny."

Whatever opinion you may have about that, I'm pretty sure we can agree that beliefs are powerful. Have you ever asked yourself why other people are so much more successful or luckier than you are? Well it has nothing to do with luck. It's because of your paradigms. The thoughts that you think and believe. Perhaps you believe some of these: You're not smart enough, you were born unlucky, you don't have the ability, only the rich can succeed, etc. Sometimes money is at the top of the list of why one is not successful or able to create the life of their dreams. True, money may play a big role, but it's not the reason. More than likely it is because of a faulty belief system. Unfortunately, like I mentioned in The Fire Within: Right Here Right Now, most of us, before and ever since we knew how to think, had our beliefs about ourselves shaped and reshaped by other people, be it peers, parents, teachers, T.V. etc. Oftentimes these beliefs are very limiting ones and are imprinted upon our minds and lives, forming our paradigms. Paradigms are a multitude of habits that are imbedded in our subconscious mind and determine how we behave or react in our lives. However, once we're able to change our thoughts we can change our lives. We each have a choice as to what we want to think and believe. Whatever it is we choose it will be real for us. It will be what our subconscious minds accept as true. In other words our beliefs are reflected right back to us like looking into a mirror. Your attitude about yourself and what you believe about your life can either create good things and great opportunities, or it can hinder opportunities and contribute to stress and aggravation. It's your choice.

Points to Remember

- Whatever your dominant thoughts are will continue to attract like thoughts

- Beliefs are one of the most powerful tools we have to shape our reality

- You already have everything you will ever need

- We each have a choice as to what we want to think and believe.

Chapter 3
The Fire Within: Thoughts

"As a man thinketh in his heart, so is he."
Proverbs 23:7

Those words are so true. It's time to learn to use your thoughts instead of being carried away by thoughts that are not conducive to the life you envision. I believe that thought is a tremendous spiritual power if used correctly. This is your life we're talking about here and you are worth enjoying it! One of the most profound concepts I ever learned is that thoughts are things. Yes, quite a remarkable statement, isn't it? What many people do not realize is that your thoughts act like magnets in that they will draw to you people, things, and of course other thoughts which are in harmony with those thoughts. Whatever thoughts you give your attention to will create or attract more of the same kind. Most of us have heard that our thoughts create our reality (although it is a mixture of thoughts and beliefs), without really actually thinking about what that implies. According to Ralph Waldo Emerson, "We become what we think about all day long." What thoughts are dominating your thinking? What thoughts do you entertain strongly? Whatever these thoughts are, they are influential, along with your beliefs and feelings, in shaping your reality. Be aware of exactly which thoughts are getting your attention. Learn to deliberately choose which thoughts you want to give your attention. Ultimately whatever you focus your thoughts and beliefs on attracts circumstances, people, and events into your life that correspond to that vibrational pattern that you are emitting or releasing. Which is to say that each and every thought will resonate with like or similar thoughts, objects, situations, and in fact, events that already exist or are coming into existence? It's like the guitar analogy. If you pluck a certain chord or string and lay another guitar facing it, the same chord will resonate. So to that end we should be mindful of the thoughts we choose to generate consciously.

Depending on the source, and there have been a few, it's been said that humans have anywhere from 40,000 to 80,000 thoughts a day. According to the "National Science Foundation NSF", it's about 50,000. Any way you look at it, that's a lot of thoughts. It has been said that as many as 80% of those thoughts have a negative component. Wow, that's not good, is it? Especially if thoughts really do create our realities. When we think the same thought over repeatedly it will eventually become a habit of thought. This thought in the long run becomes a belief, which will control the actions you take. That's why it's so important to monitor your thoughts and see just what kind of life they are suggesting or creating. We either use emotions, pictures, or words to form thoughts, which are the self-talk going on in our minds all day long. Imagine getting those under control. So whether it is positive or negative, what we continuously think and affirm becomes our belief system and creates our reality. We are usually unconsciously through our thoughts, building and confirming our belief system. Once we decide consciously to replace negative thoughts with positive thoughts and remain persistent in thinking these new thoughts, they will also build and continue to confirm our beliefs and enhance our reality until we are able to create the life that we want.

So what's the first step in controlling these thoughts? Well, you will first have to acknowledge and understand that like attracts like. You may have heard this concept in relation to the law of attraction. This is not some hocus pocus new wave concept. You may have heard about this while reading or watching **The Secret.** Think of the guitar analogy again. In simple terms positive thoughts create positive vibrations that attract positive things to you and the same thing happens with negative thoughts. Just think about it. How many times has your day started out less that alright, perhaps some unsettling incident, phone call, conversion, etc, and you continued to think about it, and then maybe said "it's one of those days", or "I'm having a bad day", or whatever can go wrong is going wrong"? Does it seem like negative things just keep escalating? It's because of the energy you're emitting. Or perhaps you have one of those days where it seems like you can do no wrong, or everything is just right with the world. Same concept. That's basically what the law of attraction is but more than that. Don't make the mistake of thinking the law of attraction is waving your hands, saying abracadabra and things magically appears. It is not a shortcut to success, although by doing the techniques I'm going to suggest and having fun doing them, it can make the path smoother and quicker. And if you understand it and learn to use it correctly, it will allow you to create your ideal life. In the process you will be rewiring your brain. Once you start focusing your thoughts more on what you do want then it will seem like magic because you WILL be receiving more of what you do want. You've spent your whole life having your belief system molded by society, peers, and media, isn't it time you chose for yourself what thoughts you want to form your beliefs, your paradigm? Remember, thoughts are real things, and if you want to create your ideal life you must first change the way you think and what you put your focus on. Remember that you have the ability to use your thoughts to create success and uncover opportunities that are right in front of you, but maybe because of negative thinking and beliefs you don't recognize these talents, abilities, and potential that you possess. Isn't it time to change that? Before you can create your ideal life, you must first change your thinking. When you focus on positive thoughts you create room in your mind for success, and once you've mastered that kind of thinking your thoughts will be in alignment with your passion and good intentions, and you will be on track to creating your ideal life.

Finally your brain is adaptable and pliant. You have the ability to shape and reshape it through taking consistent, uninterrupted action and activity over a period of 30 days or more. Depending on the behavior it's been said that the average time it takes for a new behavior to become automatic as just about sixty-six days. I know you've probably heard it said that it takes twenty-one days, however, it could take from eighteen and up to 254 days to form a new habit. But it still begins right here right now. Why wait? In the large scheme of things and looking at how long we've been thinking certain thoughts, believing certain things, and acting in certain ways, I believe it's still worth taking the time to change our thinking to create the life we wish to have.

Points to Remember

1. Thoughts are things

2. Whatever thoughts you give your attention to will create or attract more of the same kind

3. It is important to monitor your thoughts and see just what kind of life they are suggesting or creating

4. You have the ability to use your thoughts to create success

Chapter 4
The Fire Within: Gratitude

*"Gratitude is the single most important ingredient
to living a successful and fulfilled life."*
Jack Canfield

Now we come to perhaps my favorite subject, Gratitude. As I've often been quoted as saying, "It starts with gratitude, it ends with gratitude, and everything in between should be filled with gratitude, also." Gratitude is a very powerful way to achieve success in life. In fact there has been much research demonstrating that focusing on what we are grateful for is a powerful rewarding way to feel happier and more fulfilled. Gratitude also has great healing power. It actually puts us in a positive frame of mind which in turn attracts more positive things into our lives. So my suggestion is that if you're wanting more out of life and wanting less stress, then cultivate an attitude of gratitude. It attracts abundance and miracles. In fact I would strongly recommend that you make yourself a gratitude journal where you can write down each day, the things that you have to be grateful for. It may surprise you to see just how much you have going for you in your life. Just by being grateful for the things you have, no matter how small, even those things will begin to increase, and being grateful for the increase brings more increase. That's how it works. Sounds simple? It is. Like thoughts attract like thoughts. It's just getting into the repetition and persistence process of it. I can't say this enough, gratitude changes everything. What gratitude does is help us appreciate what we do have instead of always focusing on what we don't have. It enhances our abundance vibe. When we choose to see the blessing in our lives, our relationships, the food we have, wonderful memories, good times we've shared with someone, etc, that is gratitude at its best. A little gratitude goes a long way towards bringing other things to be grateful for. It actually gives me energy and inspiration and is actually the reason that I'm writing this book. Gratitude has the power to change your circumstances and change your life. Right before your eyes things begin to change, sometimes in subtle and sometimes in amazing ways. That's the magic of gratitude. Most of us have heard of the saying "count your blessings" which means focus on what you are grateful for. You also may not realize the tremendous advantages of counting your blessings and how powerful that practice is. Plus if you're not counting those positive blessings then no doubt you're counting their counterparts…negative things. And the more negative things you concentrate on the more negative things you will attract into your life. I'm sure we all know someone or have met someone who is always complaining about one thing or another. The negative energy from complaining does not promote good health or a sound mind. Let's look at health for a moment. Health is one of the most precious things we have in life but think about how much we take it for granted. Most only think about it when it begins to deteriorate. We usually don't think that much about our health unless we are sick. Without good health we could not keep our minds on the life we wish to create because we are constantly thinking of the pain for the most part. And if we continue to dwell on it, it brings negative thoughts which attract more of the same. Except for those people who live, eat, and sleep healthy. When we are grateful for our health our health will increase. Have you ever noticed when you don't feel well and you start talking about how sick you feel and the pain you're having that you start to feel worse, and when you start to talk about how great you feel you feel better, too? What if we spend some time each day thinking about and being grateful for whatever part of our health is good. It could be that we have all of our limbs, or able to breath, or able to walk, stand, jump, or whatever you have to be thankful for. Don't underestimate the power of practicing gratitude every day. Gratitude sets you on the path to success.

The daily rituals of life, work, bills, money, etc. can bring so much stress and negative thoughts. So turning our attention to what's really important, such as family, love, beauty, and great relationships are more important and spring from deep within our hearts. In the Bible it says to, "Keep thy heart with all diligence; for out of it are the issues of life.' Our hearts and minds direct everything we do, so if our hearts are full of gratitude we will see the world with love and attract other things to be grateful for. Another verse from the bible is found in 1 Thessalonians 5:16-18, "Be joyful always; pray continually; give thanks in all circumstances, for this is God's will for you in Christ Jesus." Whether are not you are religious is not the point. The point being there is something to be said for being thankful and grateful. Cultivating the habit of being grateful will eventually turn into second nature. You will remember more and more things that you have to be grateful for while attracting more things to be grateful for. Again, don't make this a chore, but be light with it and have fun. Make a game out of it and remember to smile. It makes all the difference. Right now before you read any further, stop and pause, and take a moment to ask yourself, what you are grateful for today? After a moment smile and let gratitude take you to a new way of viewing the world. Start making a conscious effort to start noticing all the wonderful things in your life and all the beautiful things in this world. Notice the things that you take for granted every day, from your breath, clothes, friends, and every other thing that you can think of that makes you smile or helps you navigate through this life. Watch as your blessing begin to multiply through gratitude. If you become a student of gratitude, life will continue to show you wonderful miracles. These miracles are happening around us always, we just miss many of them because we're busy concentrating on what we think we do not have.

Points to Remember

1. Gratitude is a very powerful way to achieve success in life

2. Gratitude also has great healing power

3. A little gratitude goes a long way towards bringing other things to be grateful for

4. Gratitude has the power to change your circumstances and change your life

5. Make a conscious effort to start noticing all the wonderful things in your life

6. Miracles are happening around us always

Chapter 5
The Fire Within: Creating Success

Success is a state of mind.
"If you want success, start thinking of yourself as a success."
Dr. Joyce Brothers

Many people think that being unsuccessful is just their fate in life and that is absolutely not true. You have to think of yourself as a success, believe in your ability to be successful, visualize yourself in a successful state, and then create your ideal life. Whatever success means or looks like to you. It has to be your idea and vision of success, not anyone else's. Creation begins with an idea, so make sure it's your idea. It will be your offspring. The thoughts associated with your idea and nurtured will increase your ability to carry out your goals. This is your destiny being created. Most people have no idea what they want in their lives or even give much consideration about what success actually means to them. And I'm not talking about someone else's definition or something obtained through the media. I've heard it said that by the time a person reaches the age of 17, approximately 150,000 times they will have heard the statement "You can't do that!" You're too young, not smart enough, not committed, don't know how, or whatever the case may be. We've all heard someone discourage their kids without really meaning to do so, with statements like, you'll never learn, or you always mess up, you always do it wrong, quit being so stupid, etc. If they hear something long enough and enough times then they will come to believe that and it will become one of those paradigms I mentioned earlier. In this day and age there are so many opportunities to create the life that you want to live. There will always be naysayers, however, they don't matter. What matters is that you believe that you can. Like Henry Ford said, "Whether you think you can or think you can't, you're right." Again, that's the power of belief, and that's what will set you on the road to success. There are no limits except the ones you impose on yourself. There are an abundance of opportunities waiting on you to open the door. There is no reason why each of us can't live a life of prosperity and abundance if we so choose. And yes, it is a choice. There is so much potential within that's waiting for expression. Waiting for you to write your very own success story. Thomas Edison has been accredited as saying, "If we did all the things we are capable of doing, we would literally astound ourselves". This is something that I truly agree with. Once a person takes responsibility for their own life and acknowledge that they are the one creating their reality, then they can be on the path to creating their own success.

Remember, success comes with a price, and in this case the price will be changing your paradigm, believing in yourself, putting energy into your vision of success, changing the way you look at things so that the things you look at change, and giving up the old unnecessary things and whatever is not conducive to your goodwill and good fortune. The price may even be giving up old friends and associates who are holding you back, or naysayers. You don't have to stop loving them, but as stated before, it s difficult to soar with eagles when you trot with turkeys.

As you start seeing yourself and feeling yourself a success in the present moment, you will attract more successful things into your life. More ideas, people, opportunities, and events will seemingly appear out of nowhere, but it will be your positive vibes attracting more things vibrating on the same positive frequency. When these things come into your life, be grateful and remember that gratitude in a little turns to gratitude in a lot. And when you feel connected to your ideal life and your vision of success, your belief system will change, your brain will be rewired so to speak, and you will be on your way, on your new journey, and traveling the path that you created. For all intents and purposes you will already be a success. Everything happens in the NOW moment.

Points to Remember

1. You have to think of yourself as a success

2. It has to be your idea and vision of success, not anyone else's

3. There are no limits except the ones you impose on yourself

4. There is so much potential within that's waiting for expression

5. Believe in yourself, put energy into your vision, change the way you look at things

6. Gratitude in a little turns to gratitude in a lot

Chapter 6
The Fire Within:
Manifesting your desires

"What you hope, you will eventually believe. What you believe you will eventually know. What you know, you will eventually create. What you create, you will eventually experience. What you experience, you will eventually express. What you express, you will eventually become. This is the formula for all of life."

Neale Donald Walsch

Now how do we create the life of our dreams? How do we manifest the things we desire? It's a process. Manifesting is when dreams become reality, and it is something that anyone can learn. It starts by taking responsibility for our own lives. It starts with individual accountability. Take a good look at where you are in your life now. Is it where you want to be? Is it where you believe you should be? Most people do not know or understand that the life that they're living has been manifested by them. It's basically created by their thoughts, feelings, and beliefs. Remember Job in the bible? Remember his statement? "For the thing which I greatly feared is come upon me, and that which I was afraid of is come unto me" (Job 3:25). You manifest what you continually focus on, worry about, and think about, especially with strong emotions behind the thoughts. Sometimes we have things that seem to keep coming up, which may seem to be random, however, maybe it's because we're not controlling your thoughts, maybe it's because you don't even know that you can control them. Is that possible? Yes, it is. As I mentioned before, it all comes down to changing your belief system. Maybe you've tried and tried to manifest the life you want with no success. Does it seem like the more you try to take a step forward you seem to take two steps backwards? Do you want it so badly that you can almost taste it? Maybe you don't really believe on a subconscious level that you can achieve it. As you believe so will you receive. Manifesting what you want is a process.

There are some tools which should be helpful. Maybe you've heard of some or all of them, but maybe you didn't believe that they were for you. Maybe you've tried some are all of them but have given up after a few days. I find that many people do it with New Year's Resolutions. Again, there are some very helpful tools to use to help transform your belief system. When manifesting you need to be clear about what it is that you want to manifest into your life. You must be clear about your intentions. In chapter 7 are some tools and techniques that should help you with your manifesting.

There really is an art to manifesting which you will discover if you just keep going. Remember to have fun as you set out on this journey. Make it enjoyable. That's what successful people do while they're manifesting success. They try different ways and enjoy the ride. As you do this you will be creating miracles in your life. So keep focusing on what you do want and not what you don't want. Like Don Miguel Ruiz stated, we're all artists creating our own art. So decide what art you want to create. You have the canvass and the tools to create. Create your own masterpiece and like artists do, enjoy the process. It can take you to extraordinary places by

implementing the techniques and tools I've suggested you should be able to accelerate your ability to create your ideal life. As a Certified Life Coach I work with individuals who want to changes the way their life is, so I often ask this question: "What would your ideal life look like?" "What would it feel like?" And I state that it won't be my ideal life but their ideal life and it will be up to them to manifest it and make it a reality. So get honest about what you want and begin right here right now. Mark Twain said, "The secret of getting ahead is getting started..." So, make a decision and make it happen.

Chapter 7
The Fire Within: Visualization

"Visualize this thing that you want, see it, feel it, believe in it.
Make your mental blue print, and begin to build."

Robert Collier

Originally, the title of this book was going to be, The Fire Within: Believing is seeing, because it all starts with belief, then it manifests into what you can see. When you create a picture of what you want your life to be and then add in belief, then you're certainly on your way. The first step is creating a vivid vision of your dream. That blueprint is what you focus on. There is tremendous power in visualizing. It has the power to transform your life. And that's the whole point of what you're trying to do, right? Visualization is a bit like meditation, however it is much more specific, directed at a certain outcome. Athletes, motivational speakers, writers, and just about any successful professional uses visualization techniques. Baseball pitchers visualize where they want to place the ball and perhaps even pitching the perfect game. Track stars visualize themselves taking off and crossing the finish line ahead of the competition. Even the late great Muhammed Ali said that he always saw himself in victory long before the match even started. When you use positive visualization techniques you're well on your way to creating that ideal life. I've heard it said somewhere that if you can't picture and visualize yourself achieving a goal or desire, then most likely you won't succeed in accomplishing it.

I've found early in the morning when I first wake and right before going to bed great times to visualize. Five to ten minutes of this is a great start. Creative visualization is the process of using your focused imagination to paint a picture in your mind of what you desire to manifest into your reality (Eintein said "Your imagination is your preview of life's coming attractions"). It's also good to bring that picture up again and again throughout the course of your day. If your picture is somewhat blurry, that's ok. It will only improve as you continue to practice. Many famous people saw their goals and dreams well before they manifested in the physical world. Picturing yourself succeeding in your mind first and watch it manifest into reality. Make sure you feel the thrill of succeeding as you imagine and visualize. You will experience the extraordinary benefits of this practice of taking time to see yourself and feel yourself where you want to be and doing what you want to be doing. Envision yourself successful and don't let that old paradigm of doubt make you give up or hold you back. Believe in yourself and keep visualizing. Use belief to power your visualization exercises. Keep your vision strong and positive while smiling at your destiny.

Visualization Technique

Step 1: Find a comfortable position

Find a comfortable spot and position. Try to avoid places that will make you sleepy, although the main thing is just to start. You could lie down or sit, although it's generally a good idea to sit, at least until you become more proficient. Sitting in an upright position will provide the best flow of breath and a good way to remain awake. There are a number of seated positions but sitting with your back again a chair or wall will take the pressure off the base of your spine and also put less pressure on your legs. Again, just getting started is the most important thing.

Step 2: See yourself where you want to be

Imagine that you are sitting comfortably in a big movie theater looking at a large screen. Imagine that the lights are low. Think about something you want to have happen. On the large screen, picture yourself in the future that you desire, doing whatever it is that you're wanting and whatever goal you're wanting to achieve. Create as much detail as you can. Are there any other people around? What are they saying? Add in any sounds you would be hearing in your ideal situation. Next, add any emotions that you think you would be experiencing as you engage in this activity, such as excitement, joy, wonder, contentment, etc. If there are any smells associated with your goal, smell them. If there is anything to touch, do so. A hug, a handshake, a podium, whatever you can imagine.

Step 3: Step into the future

Next, get up from your comfortable seat, walk up to the screen, and step through into the movie, become part of it as if it is actually happening now. Now experience the whole thing again from inside of yourself, looking out through your eyes. This is called an "embodied image" rather than a "distant image." It will deepen the impact of the experience. Again, see everything in vivid detail, hear the sounds you would hear, and feel the feelings you would feel.

Step 4: Use your senses

This step goes along with step 2 and 3. For effective visualization I recommend that you use all your senses. Your sense of sight, smell, hearing, taste, and touch will make for a clear picture. If cheering, clapping, or singing is involved, hear them with your inner ear. The same with smell, i.e. flowers, food, perfume. Use your inner sense of touch to feel a handshake, car leather, an instrument, or whatever fits your situation. Using your inner sense of taste and sight will also be very effective. Go ahead, imagine and daydream with focus. This is powerful visualization.

Points to Remember

1. The first step is creating a vivid vision of your ideal life

2. There is tremendous power in visualizing

3. Visualization should be specific, and directed toward a certain outcome

4. When you use positive visualization techniques you're well on your way to creating that ideal life

5. Envision yourself successful and don't let old paradigms of doubt make you give up

6. Keep your vision strong and positive

Chapter 8
The Fire Within: Affirmations

"My favorite affirmation when I feel stuck or out of sorts is: Whatever I need is already here, and it is all for my highest good. Jot this down and post it conspicuously throughout your home, on the dashboard of your car, at your office, on your microwave oven..."

Wayne Dyer

By now you have probably heard about affirmations. You've most likely heard that affirmations are positive statements given in the present tense that relate to what it is you want to manifest into your life. The idea is that they will become embedded in your subconscious so they can then manifest themselves in your life, given you the desired results.

What you are trying to do is pinpoint the change or goal you are trying to manifest in your life and direct your attention and focus towards it. Mostly, affirmations are for self-esteem work, however, given enough time, on their own affirmations can start to change your outlook on yourself and life a little. The thing is that if you don't believe what you're stating or writing, it will probably have little effect. However, there is one thing that most agree on and that is that affirmations are an important part of manifesting and bringing your dreams and desires from imagination to reality. The key ingredient is belief. If you feel that you are lying to yourself you will not be able to generate the desired results.

Don't worry, as I stated before affirmations do have their place in the scheme of things. I believe that affirmations are a direct communication and link with your 'Fire Within', your authentic self, and as such should always be positive and life-enhancing. Keep your affirmations clear, concise, and focused. Use them for truth and goodwill. You can either write the affirmations down or speak them. Repetition is also a key to manifesting what you're seeking. You must use these positive affirmations on a daily basis, combining them with your power of intention and an attitude of gratitude. This process will begin to rewire and reprogram your brain towards a positive way of thinking.

Points to Remember

1. Affirmations are positive statements given in the present tense that relate to what it is you want to manifest into your life

2. Affirmations become embedded in your subconscious to help manifest desired results

3. Given enough time, affirmations can start to change your outlook on yourself

4. The key ingredient is belief

5. Keep your affirmations clear, concise, and focused

6. You must use these positive affirmations on a daily basis

Chapter 9
The Fire Within: Intention

"The world is awaiting your gift - all you have to do is show up with the right intention!"

Lewis Howes

One tool that we each have at our disposal is power of confident intentions, although this is not widely known by most people. Intention will help you to have a greater chance of succeeding in manifesting your dreams and creating your ideal life. You can choose to use your power of intention to create the life, dream, or the relationship that you desire. Whenever I use good intention it creates more good things in my life, and I know that you can also use this power of intention to create the success you desire.

Like Dr. Wayne Dyer I perceive intention as a force in the universe that allows the act of creation to take place. The act of bringing things into manifestation. I don't look at intention as extreme force of effort, but as a force that is natural and inherent, indwelling, abundant, and creative. I've also learned that being playful and having fun, without becoming too attached to the outcome is an extraordinary way to manifest your dreams and obtain your goals. Also, having real desire and passion helps in the manifestation process. In the same way, intentions without desire have very little power to create. Use your intention for the things that you really care about. Use it lovingly and kindly. The more you trust the process and the more you trust, believe, and expect your intentions to manifest, the higher the probability. There are many books, DVDs, videos, etc. on Intention, and I suggest that you find what works best for you. Just know that when you begin to work with intention, you will open up a whole new world. As with the other tools I suggested, the best way to grow and learn is to actually begin. May it multiply your blessings.

Points to Remember

1. Intention is a force in the universe that allows the act of creation to take place

2. You can choose to use your power of intention to create the life that you desire

3. Intentions without desire have very little power to create

4. The more you trust the process and expect your intentions to manifest, the higher the probability

5. When you begin to work with intention, you will open up a whole new world

Chapter 10
The Fire Within:
Creating your ideal life

"Now is the time to lead your ideal life."
Phil Cousineau

At this point I'm going to give you some techniques or ideals that you can use to put you on track to creating the life that you desire. Some of these you may have heard of or perhaps even tried. Most people start off trying these and then just kind of fall away from doing them sort of like what happens after making New Year's Resolutions. Again, there's the paradigm thing. As I mentioned earlier, it takes persistence and repetition. I will tell you, that if you try these techniques and continue to practice them, they will make a wonderful difference in your life. I'm a big supporter of this quote by Napoleon Hill, "Create a definite plan for carrying out your desire and begin at once, whether you're ready or not, to put this plan into action." So now I'm going to give you some techniques to try. Be persistent with them, and have some fun applying them. If one of the techniques isn't fun and it get to be like a task, and chore, something unenjoyable, then stop it, slow down, give it a rest and try one of the techniques that makes you feel good. Feelings have a great deal to do with what you're able to manifest. Also remember that we are always manifesting. All the time whether it be, subconsciously, through our thoughts, or even what we fears. Remember the Job story from earlier? Manifesting is a real process in which we bring in things we desire. And remember that there are principles to manifesting your desires. Working with manifesting means controlling your thoughts because they create your reality. If you are able to control your thoughts, then you will be able to control what you want to manifest in your life. And by the same token, if you can't control your thoughts, things will manifest that you don't want but it will because of what you keep your mind on and your subconscious belief. Your belief system, your paradigm. So let's concentrate on what you want to manifest. Try these techniques. And of course number one on my list is:

1. Gratitude! Try keeping a gratitude journal. I keep one, and it helps me stay focused on and remember the wonderful things that I have going on in my life. Remember, gratitude in a little will become gratitude in a lot. When you stay thankful and practice gratitude, negative thought don't take over and lead you into all kinds of negative situations or depression. Try spending five minutes a day writing in your gratitude journal, but don't let it become a chore. Even one minute a day will help activate your abundance vibe. This gratitude can be for people, places, events, memories, etc. Writing in your gratitude journal will activate ideas and manifest other things in your life that you desire. So remember to have an attitude of gratitude.

2. Smile! We've all heard the expression laughter is the best medicine. I gave you the technique of smiling in my last book. Scientists have discovered that smiling on purpose can help people to feel better and actually lead you to feel happiness. It somehow changes your brain chemistry. They say that emotions originate in the brain and the muscles in our face will reinforce or transform those feeling. In Psychology Today printed that the act

of smiling activates neural messaging that benefits your health and happiness. I think if this is true then it is well worth the try, right? Plus smiling can make other people happy. Remember Lois Armstrong's song, "When you're smilin', the whole world smiles with you?" Yes, smiling is contagious. My wife has that kind of smile, and when she laughs it fills the whole room with warmth and joy. So keep smiling.

3. Intention! When you wish to manifest something, intend it. Set your intention. Intend to make it happen. Make a clear statement. Record or write it out. Make your thoughts on what you wish to manifest your dominant thoughts. First get clear on whatever it is you want to manifest. If there is strong positive emotions involved, then you are more apt to manifest what you desire. If there is no real desire behind the intention then it will be less likely to manifest. Also, when you set yourself to manifest something and negative thoughts pop into your mind, replace those thoughts with positive ones. Make a conscious choice. If a thought comes to you like "who am I to start my own company", replace it with," right now I'm taking steps to create my own company so that I can fulfill my life's dream." Remember to be Specific. Write down your intentions and be as specific as possible. Have fun with this.

4. Meditate! Another thing that I'm big on is meditation. I couldn't imagine what my life would be like without

meditation. Meditation is good for reducing anxiety, quieting the mind, relaxation, reducing stress or pain, feeling peace and calmness, and it's also been known to reduce blood pressure, and boost the body's immune system. If you haven't meditated, this should be great. Don't get too serious. I would start in a comfortable position, perhaps sitting on a cushion or chair. I would suggest closing your eyes, breathe normally, next bring your attention to your breath, notice your chest rising and falling, or notice the air moving in and out of your nose. When thoughts take you from noticing the breath, just gently bring your attention back to the breath. Don't try to fight the thoughts or get rid of them, it will only create more thoughts. The mind is busy and it's the nature of the mind to think, so be kind and gentle to your mind. Remember, in meditation there is nothing to fix, nothing to actually do. Just be and notice that sensation. After 5 or 10 minutes gently bring your attention back to your surroundings. Pause and in that moment make a conscious choice as to how you would have your day continue. There is more on meditation, but this should be a good start.

5. Visualize! Visualization is another powerful tool used in manifesting. You must first see it in your mind's eye before you see it in the physical world. First see or visualize the result or event which you wish to manifest. Set your intention to manifest this. Move your vision or imagination into the physical world. Visualize the tools

you may need to be successful. Feel how you will feel when you've manifested your desire. Remember, emotions are powerful and part of the process. While visualizing use bright colors and hear the sounds associated with having your desire. Are there people talking, singing, etc? Research shows that visualization works because neurons in our brains interpret imagery as equivalent to real-life action. More technical but that's the gist of it. Remember, success begins with a goal, so you must know and see your goal, and then it will manifest. See it, believe it, then see it manifest.

6. Affirmations! Affirmations are a big part of manifesting, also. It is good if your affirmations are infused with emotion and belief. They should be clear and short. When used correctly, affirmations are a great tool to have. They can be very effective. You've heard me speak about belief. Well the more you repeat your affirmations the more they settle into your subconscious and the more you will come to believe them. Infused with positive emotions affirmations will contribute to your dreams becoming reality. They can be written down or spoken. Like so many of the manifestation techniques, having an attitude of gratitude will work wonders in creating your ideal life. Visualize while affirming your desire, and mix them with emotions of love, joy, and happiness. Most importantly, as with the other techniques, have fun and detach yourself from the outcome. Intend, believe, smiles, and let it happen.

Points to Remember

1. Create a definite plan for carrying out your desire and begin at once

2. Remember, it takes persistence and repetition

3. Keep a Gratitude Journal

4. Set your intention

5. Meditate

6. Visualization is another powerful tool used in manifesting

7. Success begins with a goal

8. The more you repeat your affirmations the more they settle into your subconscious

Chapter 11
The Fire Within: Transformation

"Personal transformation can and does have global effects. As we go, so goes the world, for the world is us. The revolution that will save the world is ultimately a personal one."

Now we come to the crux of the matter. Transformation. The word "transformation," according to Merriam-Webster, means "a complete or major change in someone or something's appearance, form, etc." If we are wishing to create our ideal lives and change our paradigms, then transformation is needed. We leave where we were and get to where we want to be, or become what we want to become. The great mystic poet Rumi said, "Remember, the entrance door to the sanctuary is inside you." Transforming means taking hold of this very moment, in this ever present now, and deciding that you wish to be renewed, to take your future into your own hands and choose for yourself what type of life you want to create. YOUR ideal life. In order to change, we have to come to a new understanding of self and the world so that we can embrace new knowledge and have new experiences. We need to understand that it is us who have created our present reality and the world reflects back to us that which we hold in our belief system. Once we know that we can create the life we want. It's our choice what we will choose. If it's abundance you desire, then see yourself as the person who already has abundance. See yourself as abundance. And a great thing to remember is that everything we see in the physical realm began in the non-physical realm. When you decide to change your life, your job, your living arrangement, etc, expect it to happen, see it as it has happen already. Expecting it creates a new reality. Expecting, believing, and visualizing it filled with joy, while continuing to affirm it, creates a new reality, a new paradigm. But you must get started. "The journey of a thousand miles, begins with a single step" as the Chinese proverb says. Also, what kind of company are you keeping? Are they uplifting, inspiring, and wholesome? A good friend of mine use to say that it's difficult to soar with eagles when you trot with turkeys. It's up to you to decide which mindset you wish to have. Limiting or abundant. The actions we take today will create the future we want tomorrow. The transformation should be about improving and growing. It means going beyond your current comfort zone and current way of life. It could mean that you start spending time with different people, positive influencers, and maybe start going to different places. Learn to trust your intuition, that still small voice. You have to have courage to challenge your old paradigm, your old ideas and beliefs. When it gets tough don't give up or give in, but rather push forward and trust and believe in yourself. When that I can't voice tries to tell you that you can't tell it "you lie" and continue moving forward. You're in the act of changing your paradigm. You owe it to yourself to be the best you, the best version of yourself. Remember, you have the power to create your ideal life. You can be as successful and you want to be. You just have to discover your what and why. What is it that you really want and why is it that you want it?

Change isn't always a smooth transition, and in fact the former paradigm will give resistance to transformation. So put your armor on and prepare for battle. There are a few steps that I have found useful. They should help you.

1. **Be clear about what you want**

   You need to know what it is that you truly want. Be specific about what it is in your life that you want to change. Be clear and focused.

2. **Meditate on what you desire**

   Take some time to sit quietly, presumably with your eyes closed, and meditate on your desire. Gently follow your breath for a moment until you feel calm or centered. Meditation can incorporate visualizing and repeating affirmation.

3. **Visualize and Feel**

   Visualizing is using your imagination in a direct and focused manner. This is where you create the picture of your ideal life or situation. Simply create a picture of what you want to happen in your life. It may be best to imagine a big motion picture screen or t.v. screen with your desire imprinted on the screen. Be sure to add lots of vivid color, sounds, emotions and feelings. Imagine how you will feel when the desire is accomplished. Feel it as if it is already happening. Are there other people involved? What are they saying? This is where you get an opportunity to play with it until it feels right for you. Smile as you watch the movie unfold.

4. **Set your intention**

   As you make the decision to create your ideal life, as you meditate on that desire, and as you visualize what you want accomplished, set your intention and intend for it to come to pass. You mean for this to happen. When you intend there is power and flowing energy. When you are consistent change happens more quickly. Each day set your intention for what you want to create. I usually script my day on paper or by previewing my day and the way I would like for it to unfold. You will be amazed at how accurate the outcome can be. A good thing to do is let go of the outcome. It may sound like a paradox, but the more you struggle with the outcome the more resistance you will have. It's sort of like the statement to ask and then let go and let god. When you're not attached to the outcome you have more peace and opportunity to focus on other things. Set your intention and relax, smile, and go have some fun with life.

5. **The buck stops here**

This saying was popularized by US president Harry Truman, and the definition basically means that the responsibility for something cannot or should not be passed to someone else. In other words we should be the one accountable for what we allow our lives to be. At the place where I spend my time helping and mentoring young adults, one of our Core Values is Individual Accountability and I'm a big advocate of that one. Sometimes it means admitting you made a mistake, overlooked something, or was responsible for something happening. The great author and motivational speaker Jack Canfield has being accredited with the statement

"If you want to be successful, you have to take 100% responsibility for everything that you experience in your life." If you haven't already I would highly recommend his book The Success Principles. Don't make it about what happens to you, but your attitude about what happens in your life. Have the attitude of "The Buck Stops Here", and use it to encourage and make change.

Points to Remember

1. Transformation is a complete or major change in someone or something's appearance, form, etc.

2. In order to change, we have to come to a new understanding of self and the world

3. When you decide to change your life, your job, your living arrangement, etc., expect it to happen, see it as it has happen already

4. Transformation should be about improving and growing

5. Start spending time with different people and positive influencers

Chapter 12
The Fire Within: Abundance

"Abundance is not something we acquire.
It is something we tune in to."

Wayne Dyer

Yes, I also believe that abundance is something that we tune in to. It comes from within. In fact it is everywhere. It is a way of thinking. It is a way of living. When we change our paradigms we realize the potential that lies within ourselves. I remember reading somewhere that abundance is a state of mind and can't be lost, taken, or bestowed on you. It's not about what you have, but about what brings you fulfillment. If you obtain an abundance mindset it creates a shift that can actually change everything. It's not material things that brings happiness, but knowing that everything you need you already have, and that happiness comes from within. So abundance actually begins with you. Your thoughts and emotions are powerful things that have the ability to manifest things. A mindset of lack creates lack, while an abundance mindset reveals abundance. So shift your focus from what you don't have to having gratitude for what you do have, which will in return attract other things to be grateful for. True abundance is that inner knowing that your fire within, your authentic self is abundance. That old mindset and lack paradigm is not the truth. Following your purpose and passion will lead to and reveal the capacity and potential to manifest the life you want.

There is an unlimited Source of everything we could ever hope to have or manifest. It is already ours, but most of us do not know or believe it. (This is where changing paradigms becomes so important.) It is always available when we tune in to it. How do you think inventions come about, breakthroughs come about, great poetry is expressed, beautiful music is written and performed, and wonderful miracles are manifested. Yet believing in lack and putting of our attention on what is wrong or what is negative, or not believing in ourselves, actually stifles the manifestation process. Right now we are all creating the world that the next generation will inhabit. So let's leave an abundance of gratitude, compassion, love, and wellbeing. Know that you deserve abundance and do away with that attitude of not being worthy or good enough. Change that paradigm. There are ways of being in alignment. It starts with gratitude and belief. It starts with understanding that there is another way other than the way that has kept up imprisoned in a lack mindset. It is possible to envision and create a more meaningful existence, friendship, career, financial success, love relationships, etc. It starts with have the right mindset right here right now.

Points to Remember

1. Abundance is something that we tune in to

2. An abundance mindset creates a shift that can change everything

3. Your thoughts and emotions are powerful tools with the ability to manifest things

4. There is an unlimited Source of everything we could ever hope to have

5. Abundance starts with gratitude and belief

Chapter 13
The Fire Within:
Right Here Right Now

*"Time goes on. So whatever you're going to do, do it. Do it
now. Don't wait."*

Robert De Niro

The title of my last book The Fire Within: Right Here Right Now, suggested that we each have a fire that is within and it is ready to create and burn bright right here right now. Sometimes we get into a habit of waiting when we should be doing. Success starts right now, with intention, with belief, with taking that first step now. That is when things begin to happen and things begin to change.

The power of now is amazing when creating your ideal life. The power of now is transformative. Everything that has happen to you and everything in the universe has come together and brought you to this point so that you can create the reality you desire and deserve. Many people sit around and watch other people's ships come in. They watch others succeed, create, shine, and do all the things that they wish they could do. I know that patience can be virtue, however, you've also heard that there's no time like the present. Successful people are known to take action and make their dreams come true. Sure they do the research and make the plans, and visualize, and all of that, but they also get started. Even if there is some fear, they dive right in and make it happen. And unless you take that first step you will always be there dreaming while others create. The life you've been dreaming about is there waiting for you to stop waiting. So, don't miss your opportunity. Create your opportunity. See your opportunity, and be your own opportunity.

Seize the moment right here right now. Don't live with the regret of not allowing your purpose and passion to shine through. Life really happens in the now moment. Don't anticipate trouble or let doubt stifle you, but live in the moment of creating your ideal life. Live your life consciously as you contribute your fire to the world, as you allow your dream to unfold. Too often we just give up on our dreams when we should be allowing our passion to help make this world a better place. Let your success start now. Put your focus on manifesting the life you desire. Put your focus on what you do want not on what you do not want. Sure, other things may require your attention, but the things you focus on most are the things most likely attracted into your life.

Each of us is the only one who can create our best life. Each individual must take it upon themselves to make it happen. Don't regret not doing the things that you dream of doing because of old negative and outdated paradigms. Let's use our extraordinary imaginations to create a better future and a better world. Let's contribute our dreams to the world because they want to manifest into reality. What story are you ready to tell the world. What are you ready to change? It's time to be brave and have courage. Allow your authentic self to blossom and express magnificence. With your goal in mind always, live a life of gratitude and watch the blessings manifest. As you go about your day, don't forget to smile and appreciate each moment. Don't wait for life to happen, it's already happening and you're the artist to paint the picture that you wish to create. As you create you live, now. Then you will come to realize that life is happening for you not to you. Remember, don't wait for your dreams to come true or your goals to be complete to be happy. Happiness starts right here right now and it comes from within. That is the key. If we're waiting for persons, places, and things to make us happy, then we are going to be like the dog chasing his own tail. People, places, and things can be enjoyable, but nothing will satisfy unless we allow and experience the happiness from within. Don't fret if this seems an impossible task. Just keep changing those old paradigms about happiness until you realize that that which you are seeking is already within you. As expressed by St. Francis of Assisi, "The One you are looking for is the One who is looking" The Fire Within is more than a concept. It is about realization and transformation. This fire inside of us IS us. It wishes to express and grow and contribute to the growth and betterment of this planet. The fire connects all of us together even if we don't realize it. Whenever we help or have compassion for another being it spreads and grows. It makes each of us better. It helps transform this entire planet even as we each create our ideal lives. The Fire Within exits…Right Here Right Now. Use it to transform your life.

Chapter 14
The Fire Within: Power

"The life of your dreams has always been closer to you than you realized, because The Power-to have everything good in life-is inside you"

Rhonda Byrne

I absolutely love those words by Rhonda Byrne. Whenever I read those words there is a truth that I feel within me stirring. Are you following your heart and making your dreams come true by following your passion? If that is your endeavor you'll gain power, grow, and contribute your unique gift to this world. The Power that allows you to accomplish these things and be who you were always meant to be and to live your ideal life is linked to The Fire Within. You create your ideal life with your power by allowing The Fire Within to surface.

This power has been called many things such as The Force, even Love. The main thing is that we each have the power to rise from all sorts of obstacles or misfortunes. The potential to alter the way we see and view the world becomes manifest when using this power. This power allows you to bounce back when you're feeling down, disappointed, or dissatisfied.

By using the techniques mentioned in the earlier chapters, you will come to recognize and feel this power, which will help you in creating the life that you deserve. By using this power you will set in motion change and miracles to not only help you, but to also contribute to the well-being and betterment of our world. Each of us has this responsibility. Each of us has the power to add to the growth of this planet.

Learn about this power, understand this power, unveil this power, and use this power for good, to manifest a better life, and create a better future. May your Fire burn always bright.

About the author

Charles L Ellis is the author of The Fire Within: Right Here Right Now, and lives in San Diego, CA, where he endeavors to change the lives of its youth and young people. Charles believes that every person has the ability to create the life that they want. He has won numerous awards for Leadership, Language of Change, Morals and Values, Making a Difference, Above and Beyond, and others.

His focus has been on help those with non-traditional work habits and histories to seek, obtain, and maintain gainful employment. He also focuses on helping at-risk youth, to believe in themselves while growing and preparing to become productive members of society. His 'outside the box' techniques and thinking are a major reason he's had amazing success and has gained the respect of those who have come to know him.

Charles is a Certified Life Coach, Motivational Speaker, Poet and Humanitarian who uses his time to write, speak, and create online content to inspire and motivate. Charles has helped many others obtain gainful employment while changing the way they think. His mantra is, "Gratitude, I wouldn't have it any other way."

73620197R00053

Made in the USA
San Bernardino, CA
07 April 2018